Management Consulting for Rookies:

A Rookies Guide to Management Consulting

Maurice Ekpong, FIMC. CMC ®

Dedication

Dedicated to God, for the benefit of humanity. My special appreciation goes to my dear wife Tolulope and our wonderful kids Jedidiah and Hadassah. Their unrelenting support has made my experience possible.

Copyright © 2024 by Maurice Ekpong, FIMC. CMC ®

All rights reserved.

First international market edition: July 2024

Published by African Journal for Sustainable Development

www.ajsd.org

To contact the author:

E-mail: maurice.ekpong@aol.com

LinkedIn: https://www.linkedin.com/in/maurice-ekpong/

TABLE OF CONTENTS

Chapter		Page Number
Foreword –	*Professor David Iornem*	5
Review –	*Professor Francoise Cros*	6
1. Buckle up, it's a rough ride!		7
2. You don't need to know everything to find the answer		13
3. Eat your own shit!		17
4. Pick cherries along the way		21
5. Develop a cross-functional perspective		24
6. Don't sell to morons		27
7. Eat the brains of others		31
8. Go against the grain		34
9. Have a long-term perspective		37
10. Toolkit for Consultants		40

Appendix

I.	Bibliography	47
II	List of Tables and Figures	48
III	About the Author	49

and had requested for a meeting to discuss a way out of the stagnation he was experiencing at the time. We met at a Protea Hotel in Victoria Island where he spent over two hours pouring out his frustrations. I dutifully noted down all the points he made and promised to send him a proposal detailing how we may jointly approach the problem after a firsthand visit to his businesses. At the end of the meeting, I went ahead researching the challenges he had highlighted in preparation for a site visit in two weeks. This visit enabled me develop a road-map for restructuring the organization which Mr. Ernest assented to. This was the easy part.

The difficult part was implementing the road-map, in view of human resistance to change from the ownership down to the rank and file of the organization. In Nigeria, successful sole proprietors are sometimes their own stumbling blocks, limiting the capacity of their businesses to survive beyond the first generation. There are therefore very few Nigerian organizations that are in their third generation because of this as well as other factors that include lack of effective succession planning. But let's leave the other factors for another day. Suffice it to say that you will meet different shades of challenges along the way. Your problem-solving skill as a management consultant will therefore come in very handy.

Between 2012 and 2014, I was consulting for a multinational's expansion plans in Nigeria and Gabon. The organization had existing oil palm plantations in Edo State Nigeria but was looking to expand eastwards in the country. At the same time, they were developing over 20,000 hectares of palm plantation in the Republic of Gabon. Between the Group CEO who was Indian, the French COO and myself, we had put in bids to acquire brownfield oil palm estates from two of Nigeria's State Governments. Both bids were successful, given my client a combined 25,000 hectares of moribund plantations across two states. Among others, my role included stakeholder engagement, recruitment, and training of about 1,000 workers.

To give the host community the opportunity to participate, I made the point to recruit locals into my team including a Chief and his assistant. Chief Bernard used to be the Manager of the estate and so was a repertoire of the history of the plantation. He was therefore going to add value to the project. One time, while engaging with the host

Chapter One: Buckle up, it's a rough ride!

"The higher you go, the hotter it gets" – Maurice Ekpong

What the heck does management consulting mean and who is a management consultant?

I have been asked this question more times than I can remember over the past twenty years. Think of it as the conductor of an orchestra who brings a unified vision to the music while working with the orchestra to make that vision come alive. In this sense, management consulting is the practice of working with businesses to improve their performance. The management consultant therefore is the person that facilitates the process that enables businesses improve their performance. This is a very important role on many levels. First, business owners and employees after a while tend to lose perspective not unlike the homeowner who after a while fails to notice the cobwebs in the home. It sometimes takes an outsider visiting to draw their attention to the problem. Under normal circumstances, the homeowner will thank the visitor and afterwards get on with the task of clearing out the cobwebs. Now, see the homeowner as the business and the visitor as the management consultant. The only difference is that in practice, the consultant will be paid for pointing out the cobwebs.

Management consultants are therefore in high demand in all sectors: government, manufacturing, services, education, agriculture, technology, entertainment, etcetera. Any industry you can think of requires the help of management consultants in one role or the other. The consultants reward, will be directly proportional to the scale of the challenge, and the client's perception of the value the consultant brings to the table.

While this sounds dandy and exciting, the path towards becoming a successful management consultant may not be as rosy. Depending on the time zone you are operating from, there are peculiar challenges you might encounter. This is why you must buckle up for the turbulence ahead!

Sometime in 2009, a client of mine in Lagos Nigeria introduced me to an acquaintance of his who had a string of businesses in Port Harcourt. Mr. Ernest was going to be in Lagos

Book Review

This very concise 48-page guide is aimed at beginners interested in pursuing careers in management consultancy. The author walks readers through different scenarios, using humorous advice and world-class illustrative anecdotes.

The chapter titles are punchy and youthful in appearance, completely in keeping with the language of the new generation. These titles are sometimes even provocative like "you don't need to know everything to find the answer" or even more strongly "eating your own shit". These striking chapter titles nevertheless carry valuable and very serious advice, masterfully illustrating the skills necessary for the aspiring management consultant who wants to help an organization become more efficient.

We see that this advice comes from a very competent author who has experienced a very wide variety of situations; even the most difficult when company staff, for example, are hostile to a management consultant. He also made the important point that technical knowledge alone may not ensure success, when the advisor lacks the situational intelligence to motivate the company concerned. It is clear from the chapter on "eat your own shit" that the advisor must be above board.

This guide provides all kinds of very useful advice, applicable in all sectors including government, business, services, education or culture. It therefore addresses the skills, techniques but above all the "soft skills" to be utilized by any advisor seeking to be efficient in management consultancy.

We can only thank Maurice Ekpong for this work, which is truly a bible for any young person wishing to engage in the profession of management consultancy.

University Professor Françoise Cros

National Conservatory of Arts and Crafts, Paris (France)

Written in Paris, July 26, 2024

Foreword

In today's rapidly changing world, the role of management consultants faces inevitable challenges in the context of change management. Economic entities are emerging daily and encountering a multitude of risks that often lead to their untimely demise. This situation calls for an increasing number of consultants to develop solutions that can support the global economic system.

The ever-changing nature of business and government operations creates a growing demand for consultants to develop effective solutions. This has led to an increasing number of new consultants entering the field. However, some of these new consultants may lack the necessary knowledge and experience. **Maurice Ekpong** has used the term "rookies" to refer to these individuals who are just starting out in the field of consulting.

In his desire to support new entrants into the consulting field, **Maurice Ekpong** has created a masterpiece that is highly beneficial not only to rookies but also to experienced professionals. One of the book's strengths is its easy-to-read style, accompanied by real-life stories that enhance the reader's understanding of the concept of management consulting. It is my great pleasure to write the foreword to this important work produced by the brilliant professional **Maurice Ekpong**.

I am confident that this work will serve as a trusted companion and guide, helping you unlock your full potential as a management consultant, whether you are a rookie or an experienced professional. On behalf of the Institute of Management Consultants-Nigeria, I recommend this book to all consultants in Nigeria and abroad.

Prof David Iornem, Harvard University Business School Executive Program (2021) with Distinction. PhD, MSc, M.eCom, MBA(eCom), B.Sc, BAM, B.Ed, MCIM, FIMC, FCIM, FIPFM,FNIMN, Dip.M, Dip.CAM, Dip.Com, DMS, CMC, FNIM, MBIM, M.CAM, FCMA, FAICL, FCALM, MSPMC, MMS, frpa, PGDE, LTTC E-Learning, D.Litt., SEC Licensed, CIS Licensed, CFA, FCPFC, ACBAN, FCCB, Cert.AI.

Director General
Institute of Management Consultants-Nigeria.

communities, a young man who lived there invited us to his local government about 20 kilometers away to sensitize youths about the work opportunity. He thought people from his own community can benefit from the proposed project.

We heeded the plea of the young man and agreed a date to visit his community. While my team and I were carrying out the sensitization exercise 20 kilometers from the project site, an apparently angry man disrupted the meeting, asking us to leave. We thanked him and left for the local government office to notify officials of our mission and request they spread word of the opportunity to their constituencies, only to find out while there that the angry man had reported us to local police as suspected human traffickers.

If you are in a third world country, illiteracy, corruption and police brutality combine to create a toxic operating environment. The overzealous local police acting merely on sentiment, refused to look at all the documentation and ID cards we presented and promptly put my entire team in a cold cell in their station for more than 48 hours, without access to our phones. Thankfully, I had made a call before my phone was seized. It took the intervention of the Inspector General of police in Abuja to make the local Divisional Police Officer realize the huge mistake he had made; but only after the injustice was meted out to my team. Meanwhile, the state-run newspaper had published a false and unverified story about human traffickers that were apprehended!

I instructed my lawyers to sue the newspaper, local government authority and the Nigeria police force for defamation of character but after much delayed tactics by the defendants, the court ruled that the case was statute barred, because the time within which government officials could be sued had elapsed. When I visited the commissioner of police in the state capital afterwards, his appeal included a statement that anyone seeking to do great things will often face challenges.

True, the management consultant seeking to do great things must be prepared for a rough ride, especially if the operating environment is toxic. This reinforces the need for the consultant to be aware of the peculiarities of his operating environment and provide required mitigants to real and apparent risks.

One of the most devastating air crash incidents in aviation history involved Korean airlines flight 801which took off from Gimpo International Airport, Seoul headed for Antonio B. Won Pat International Airport in Guam on August 6, 1997. The Boeing 747-300 operating the flight crashed on Bijia Peak south of Nimitz Hill while approaching the destination airport killing 229 of the 254 people on board.

The U.S. National Transportation Safety Board (NTSB) investigated the incident, and among many errors identified, questioned why the first officer and flight engineer did not challenge the captain for his errors. There was already a program run by the airline to promote an atmosphere encouraging first officers and flight engineers to challenge the captain if they felt concerned. Data retrieved and analyzed from the black box revealed that the challenge on this fateful day came barely six seconds before the crash – a little too late. (NTSB, 1997)

The Korea Air crash was not an isolated case, but one of several which mirrored a systemic problem caused by a culture that prohibited juniors from challenging the authority of seniors. Since then, there have been concerted efforts led by change consultants to make for a convivial atmosphere for mutual respect. The impact of course is seen in the improvement in safety in Asian skies.

Problems like the above are typical, and come in different shades across many industries and time zones. Like the NTSB, consultants help organizations make sense of the problem, creating road-maps through a process of consensus to mitigate risks and resolve challenges. In aviation, little problems can be fatalistic. It can be no less fatalistic in the food services or healthcare sectors where a safety problem can lead to potentially fatal consequences.

According to a report by Reinhard Burger published by the National Library of Medicine, "in the summer of 2011 Germany experienced one of the largest outbreaks of a food-borne infection caused by enterohaemorrhagic Escherichia coli (EHEC) with the stereotype 0104:H4. A large number of cases with bloody diarrhea and haemolytic uraemic syndrome (HUS) occurred. Never before was such a high rate of HUS cases observed in an outbreak caused by a food-borne pathogen." The outbreak caused widespread panic and paranoia among the population because of food safety concerns. (National Academies Press (US); 2012).

This is no less serious than the case of a faulty part at the Grôna Lund amusement park in Stockholm which caused the tragic death of one person while injuring nine others on June 25, 2023. Swedish accident investigators reported one year after the accident that the country's oldest amusement park didn't properly test new parts before installation. (Reuters, 2023)

Imagine for a moment that a consultant had recommended either the disease-borne food in Germany or the equipment supplier in Sweden (without due diligence) so you can appreciate the risks to the consultant, the company and general public when anyone in the chain drops the ball. Management consulting is therefore neither for the fainthearted nor for the frivolous. To succeed you need to have the attitude and aptitude worthy of an orchestra conductor.

Always ask yourself, will my intervention crash this airplane or keep it safely in the skies? Will it enhance health and wellness of end-users or create sickness and paranoia? Will it derail the wheels of a roller coaster with fatalities or joyfully entertain holiday makers? As a consultant, your decisions have consequences. Buckle up for the ride!

Key Learning Points:

1. Management consulting is the practice of working with businesses to help improve their performance
2. The management consultant is like the conductor of an orchestra who facilitates the process that enables businesses improve their performance
3. Patiently listen to the client and take notes
4. Don't rush to proffer solutions until you have thoroughly investigated the problem
5. Write a proposal with a road-map for addressing the challenges and get the client to sign-off
6. Be ready for surprises as the assignment may not go as you anticipated
7. Know that your decisions have consequences

Action Plan

Chapter Two: You Don't Need to Know Everything to Find the Answer!

"Sometimes, the question is more important than the answer" – Maurice Ekpong

The above quote is often true in a world in a rush for answers to every problem. No doubt, the problems in the world are legion: unemployment, crime, mass migration putting pressure on limited resources, climate change and so forth. It is my belief that the answer if found, may not help the person or organization that has lost the question. Many organizations are therefore more imperiled by a loss of their raison d'être and may be better served by simply asking themselves what they exist for.

As a management consultant, the right questions in your kitty are your super power. While asking the wrong questions is bad, asking no questions at all is worse as it paints the picture of a hubristic persona. You can't afford this sort of characterization and will be well served by planning well in advance of any client meeting and preparing a question bank as a discussion guide.

One time while I was in secondary school around the 1990s, I accompanied my late dad to the farm in Ogoja Nigeria. It was the dry season and the rivers and streams were low on water, so I could easily cross the streams that straddled our ancestral farm lands. Off I went, without a machete; just lazing about approximately 300 yards from everyone. While I waited, quietly taking in the scenery, a horde of greater cane rats numbering more than fifty began moving towards me. In Africa, this number of greater cane rats or grasscutters are seldom seen by people who hunt them for meat. But here I was, young, inexperienced and unprepared for opportunity.

Likewise, it is fatalistic for the management consultant to be unprepared. While you may not have the answer to every organization's problem (and you aren't really expected to), you should be able to lead the organization to the eureka moment where they rediscover their mojo.

As a management consultant, one skill that serves you well is research. This is the ability to investigate problems. Typically, the researcher starts with a background to the subject of investigation, identifies the target audience, sets out a hypothesis, asks pertinent questions and goes all out to find answers to the questions through unbiased data gathering and analysis. While you may not need to know everything, you need to know how to know everything!

After more than twenty years as a multidisciplinary consultant working on local and multinational projects for organizations across many time zones, I still don't approach any problem with overconfidence. I sometimes have butterflies in my stomach that keep me on my toes; however always certain that I can get the desired results by following a clear road-map and asking the right questions. This will serve you well.

While it may be true that you can start from the answer and walk back to the problem, I have made the point that many times, that answer you are starting from may actually be the problem. Get back to the basics by redirecting the client to the horizon. The experienced mariner focuses on the horizon when the sea is turbulent to maintain stability. The horizon is the reason the business exists.

In 2021, a French multinational company called while I was working on a project in Nigeria's Niger Delta region to ask if I will like to join them on a proposed Pan African project they had applied for. Two weeks later, I was appointed as National Consultant for a UNESCO funded study investigating the state of Play and Prospects for the digital transformation of TVET and the skills development systems in Africa. This project was very important to UNESCO, the African Union, the World Bank, the African Development Bank and other multilateral institutions; providing baseline information for the African Unions strategic skills development plan for the continent by 2030.

In this role, I was responsible for the West African Regional Economic Community; with other colleagues from Chad, France, Madagascar, Rwanda and Tunisia. This role was for experts in education and ICT and required professional communication skills in English and French. I was neither an education nor ICT professional and my French speaking skill is still quite rusty – to put it modestly. All meetings and reports were conducted in

French, requiring that I work twice as hard as everyone else, being the only team member, whose country was mostly English speaking.

At the end of the day, my first draft report was accepted without corrections, while those of my colleagues, who were education and ICT professionals, were returned for correction several times. My report was also adjudged the most comprehensive, leading the French multinational to request that I guide one of their interns studying for a master's degree who was interested in my data. My super power was simply the road-map I had, and the right questions in my tool box.

No person exemplifies the indomitable human spirit like famous German composer Ludwig Van Beethoven. In spite of losing his hearing in his 20s, Beethoven continued making music, earning the reputation of one of the most revered figures in the history of western music. In spite of his handicap, he found his way.

The management consultant is therefore not one to whine about the weather, the political economy or his or her physical or emotional circumstance. The obstacle keeping your client's business from blossoming can't be insurmountable. Just know you can find answers to every problem if you look hard enough. You don't need to know everything or to have everything together. If you look in the right places with the right attitude, you will find the answer!

When Venetian Marco Polo set sail from Europe to Asia in 1271, he was to a large extent venturing into relatively unknown territory. His account of the Orient provided the western world with the clearest picture at the time, of the geography and customs of the East. Similarly, venturing into consultancy or taking a brief from a client is very much like sailing into the unknown. Once you have a map and a compass, you are very likely to arrive at your destination.

A map typically is a diagrammatic representation showing the relationship of elements like space, land or sea. It can be used as a tool for navigating from one point to another. For the consultant, each problem you seek to solve can be mapped out. What are the key elements of the problem you are trying to address? What are the relationships between the elements? What is the expected outcome? And how can you navigate efficiently from point A to point Z? These among others, are genuine questions that can help you make sense of the challenges in the assignment at hand. The closer to reality your map, the closer you are to effectively navigating the problem.

I encourage organizations to engage in scenario planning and visualization. You are closer to a solution when you can reduce or eliminate the fog in the room. Imagine the difference between walking a tightrope with a blind fold and walking with your eyes wide open. In a sense, the consultant is the eye of the company. Keep your eyes wide open.

Key Learning Points

1. Start from the question, not the answer
2. Prepare questions well in advance of any client meeting
3. Research is an important skill to have
4. Reduce or eliminate the fog in the room
5. Remember that while you may not need to know everything, you need to know how to know everything

Action Plan

_____
_____
_____
_____
_____
_____
_____
_____
_____
_____

Chapter Three: Eat Your Own Shit!

"Who you are speaks so loudly, I cannot hear what you are saying" – Emerson

Many consultants don't take their own medicine. This is tragic on many levels because the client can see right through you. If you can't eat your own shit, why should you serve it to others? I have seen many 'time management experts' show up late for personal effectiveness training sessions. You will agree that that isn't an effective way to improve the performance of people within an organization. To be an effective management consultant, I have found that clients will first of all need to accept your person, before they can wholeheartedly accept what you have to say. If you don't look like what you are saying, you may be better off in comedy.

Coprophagous animals like rabbits, hamsters, termites and hares sometimes feed on their own faecal matter. While this may be considered grotesque and disgusting to humans, the established practice of eating poop in the animal kingdom may have some merit, perhaps enabling them access nutrients they couldn't digest on the first try.

One day, a pigeon invited a stray dog she had met in the woods over for lunch. The dog traversed mountains and streams and finally got to the pigeons' house after running nonstop for three hours. Upon arrival, the pigeon asked the dog to eat her droppings while she feasted on the cob of corn the farmer had left out in the sun. Hungry and angry, the dog pounced on the pigeon and had her for lunch instead!

This allegorical story while unlikely to happen verbatim, paints an extreme picture of the contradictions the client may feel when a management consultant doesn't appear to believe or live out what he dishes out. Be very clear in your mind if you want to succeed in this profession that you will practice what you preach. If you do this, you will become a walking signage that self-advertises.

Too many cases abound of management consulting firms and management consultants that have wrecked businesses and self-imploded as a result of what I term corporate schizophrenia. Remember the Enron scandal? This unfortunate scandal was orchestrated by a series of events involving dubious accounting practices, resulting in the 2001 bankruptcy of Enron Corporation and the subsequent dissolution of the accounting firm Arthur Andersen on August 31, 2002; then one of the top 5 accounting firms in the world with over 85,000 partners and staff.

Simply put, Arthur Andersen didn't eat its own shit and got eaten up in the process. As a management consultant, you must maintain your integrity at all times and adhere strictly to the very high standards expected of management consulting professionals. Although not exhaustive, the minimum standards endorsed by the International Council of Management Consulting Institutes (ICMCI) include the following:

"Confidentiality
A member will treat client information as confidential and will not take personal advantage of privileged information gathered during an assignment, or enable others to do so

Unrealistic Expectations
A member will refrain from encouraging unrealistic expectations or promising clients that benefits are certain from specific consulting services

Commissions / Financial Interest
A member will neither accept commissions, remuneration or other benefits from a third party in connection with recommendations to a client without the client's knowledge and consent, nor fail to disclose any financial interest in goods or services which form part of such recommendations

Assignments
A member will accept only assignments for which the member has the skills and knowledge to perform.

Conflicting Assignments
A member will avoid acting simultaneously (in potentially conflicting situations) without informing all parties in advance that this is intended

Conferring with Clients

A member will ensure that before accepting any engagement, a mutual understanding of the objectives, scope, workplan and fee arrangements is established and any personal, financial or other interests which might influence the conduct of the work are disclosed

Recruiting

A member will refrain from inviting an employee of a client to consider alternative employment without prior consent with the client

Approach

A member will maintain a fully professional approach in all dealings with clients, the general public and fellow members

Code of Professional Conduct

A member will ensure that other management consultants carrying out work on the members behalf, are conversant with and abide by the Code of Professional Conduct"

These codes of conduct, when adhered to are fail-safe, keeping the consultant and the industry he serves above board. Ignoring them creates a tsunami sure to wipe out everything in its pathway. A reminder of the 2004 tsunami might help. It was 07.59 AM local time when a major earthquake measuring 9.1 on the Richter scale struck off the west coast of northern Sumatra in Indonesia. This undersea earthquake is reported to have been caused by a rupture along the fault line between the Burma and Indian plates. It created a tsunami of epic proportions with waves up to 100 feet high, devastating communities along the coasts of the Indian ocean and killing an estimated 227,000 people across 14 countries. (Britannica,2023)

To be sure, some of the world's recessions have been caused by the refusal of people in trust positions to adhere to ethical conduct. Elisa Desousa in a report titled 'The Ethical Dilemmas Behind the 2008 Global Financial Crisis' had this to say: "It is generally understood that ""successful companies governed by professionals with ethically rooted principles raise the standard"" and the world prospers as a result. (Thomas, 2016). Yet, historical examples of wrongful business practices are extensive, and the Global Financial Crisis of 2008 that nearly collapsed the global economy is a recent prime example of how compounded unethical choices, executed by professionals whose ethical principles lacked any moral bearings, can negatively impact and falter society."

Think of this for a minute. Not unlike the 2004 tsunami that wreaked havoc across 14 countries, a global economic tsunami might just be triggered by the inordinate ambition of a few persons in one remote corner of the globe; leading to the decimation of economies, while increasing poverty, death and inequality around the world. As a management consultant, will your conduct compound with those of others to create such a tsunami?

Key Learning Points

1. Practice what you preach
2. Avoid all contradictions
3. Maintain the highest professional standards
4. Ask yourself, what are the unintended consequences of my conduct?

Action Plan

_____
_____
_____
_____
_____
_____
_____
_____
_____

Chapter Four: Pick Cherries Along the Way

"If you go into the woods after butterflies, it won't hurt to pick cherries along the way" – Maurice Ekpong

This chapter leads to the next where I will write on the need for a consultant to have a cross functional perspective. Here however, I will encourage you to keep an open mind for fresh insight and new opportunities along your way. Don't be boring. Many times, the big picture comes from tiny pieces of a puzzle you pick up over time. If you ignore small and sometimes seemingly inconsequential clues, you may wake up one day and that tiny bit of information is all you need to solve a gargantuan riddle. Always remember that big doors swing on small hinges. Never forget.

A certain man needed money to embark on a big project and for a while couldn't quite figure out how to get it. While walking back home one day, he had a nudge to buy a dump site close to his house. He had enough money to buy the site but didn't see any use for it. As the nudge refused to dissipate, he asked to see the owner with whom he negotiated and made a down payment. Not long afterwards, a company called to buy him out for an outrageously higher amount of money. According to company officials, they desperately needed that site! You guessed right. He sold and had more than enough for his big project!

Of course, many inconsequential things remain just that: inconsequential. As a consultant however, you need to develop a kind of sixth sense; that still small voice, that sort of cancels out the loud noise of your vociferous five senses. This sixth sense may serve you very well in the days ahead.

Over the years, I have had the unique privilege of meeting people and organizations from different parts of the world. Like every mixed multitude, some organizations are not worth the paper their name is printed on. They may or may not be serious time wasters. Remember that as a consultant, you are paid for your time. Don't fritter away that time, but spend most of it on what gives you the greatest value. I am not talking here about money. While money remains an important measure of value, we are well served to understand that real value goes beyond money. It is your contribution to the human cause, what you will be remembered for long after you are gone. Because nature and the world operate on fixed principles, what you give will always return back to you in multiple fold. You will find that this sort of perspective is important for the management consultant.

Around 2007 I had a client who didn't pay much. He will ask me to help with different projects pro bono and I felt obliged to help any way I could. One day, he asked me to research for smallholder processing mills for one of the state governments in Nigeria. I got online and found a few equipment processors in Europe and China to whom I sent out email inquiries. One of the responses I got was from a British company that was about to establish a demonstration mill in Abrafo Ghana. They invited me to the launch of their mill in Ghana so I can have firsthand experience of their technology. I gave the feedback to my client who never took it forward and so I decided to proceed to Ghana regardless. From that singular visit to Ghana in 2007, the British company and I have maintained a relationship to date and from some of their referrals, I have networked and consulted for other organizations. This is not an isolated case I must say.

There are also a number of cases with time wasters. Some years ago, the CEO of a big Asian financial services company reached out to me seeking advice on market entry into Africa. Based on my understanding of the African market, I reached out to a public sector contact in Liberia to set up meetings with the government; with a gentlemanly understanding that I will be kept in the loop. Once I linked up the parties, I didn't hear from them again. You might say I should have signed non-circumvention agreements with both parties, blah blah blah! I know, and I am quite an expert at drafting agreements etcetera but honestly, if I can't do business with someone over a handshake, they aren't worth my time.

As a consultant, understand that building the right relationships takes time. You must therefore identify those relationships carefully and nurture them tenderly. As you pick up cherries along your way, you may find that some that look really good from a distance aren't that good close up. Conversely, others that aren't that attractive from a distance may be worth your time eventually. It's your call. Whatever time you chose to spend with either good or bad cherry, ensure you leave them better off. Nature has a way of rewarding you, even for wasting your time with good intentions!

The diamond mines of Golconda are reported to be one of the biggest diamond finds in history. In the book 'Acres of Diamonds', a tale is told of a Persian called Ali Hafed who sells his house to travel the world in the relentless search for diamonds. He becomes poor and dies in the process never realizing that the house he sold had acres of diamonds in his backyard, making the new owner extremely rich. The new owner picked up a cherry abandoned by Alii Hafed, literarily striking diamond in the process. Be careful what you pick up or leave behind on your consulting journey. Will it end up as a diamond mine or an abandoned house?

Key Learning Points

1. Keep an open mind for fresh insight and new opportunities
2. Remember that big doors swing on tiny hinges
3. As a consultant, you need to develop a sixth sense
4. As a consultant, you are paid for your time. Don't waste it!
5. You will always get back the value that you give. Nature ensures that
6. Building the right relationships takes time

Action Plan

Chapter Five: Develop a Cross-Functional Perspective

"A cursory examination of humankind tends to lend credence to an innate ability in the individual to do multiple things successfully through diligence and practice" – Maurice Ekpong

While specialization is good, the modern world of work in view of the third industrial revolution with its inbuilt system of constant disruption from the impact of automation, robotics, artificial intelligence and the internet of things is best served by an agile orientation. This being the case, cross-functional teams separated across different time zones and geographies will take an increasingly prominent place in the way leading companies structure themselves this century. The response time to address concerns on a client's project, or to ship out a product or service to the end user may define who takes a leading share of markets around the world. That said, nimble companies no matter how young or small will continue to upset apple carts across all industries, leading to an increased demand for restructuring and re-organization consultancy for small and large corporates this decade and beyond. To make the point clearer, just remember what Uber has done to traditional car hire companies like Avis and Hertz since its founding in March 2009 or what cell phone cameras did to Kodak forcing it to declare bankruptcy in 2012. Knowledge of these types of cases will certainly keep you grounded in reality as you engage with your clients.

The catalytic change in the world of work from the impact of technology is both an opportunity and a threat to the management consultant. As computers become more efficient at crunching incredible volumes of data in record time, the consultant must up his game to remain relevant in this changing scheme of things. The trite adage that says no knowledge is lost still rings true. You must deliberately seek to understand how different related or unrelated parts of a system impact performance, and thereby develop ways to optimize the system.

Over the past twenty-something years, I have worked in different roles across multiple sectors: agriculture, financial services, healthcare, transportation, infrastructure, oil and gas, real estate, education, media, manufacturing, nonprofits, name it. My role has been legion including marketing, business development, stakeholder engagement, project management, human capital development, research etcetera. Because of the different sectors I have worked in and roles I continue to play, I have gained a sort of helicopter perspective; enabling me empathize with the different functions of a work system. This is quite useful in the emerging world of work.

While you may rightly choose to specialize, the thrust of this epistle is to put you on notice that in the last five minutes, something could have changed in the world of work that you must pay attention to. Perhaps a new product, service or technology may have been introduced somewhere in this vast world of ours that can disrupt your client's business with significant consequences. Stay abreast of the trends and don't let your client become another Kodak!

One fascinating childhood poem is of the six blind men of Indostan by John Godfrey Saxe. The poem masterfully satirizes human perception and the limitations of knowledge. To each, the elephant was merely like the part of the body he could touch and feel. The truth is that everyone had a piece of the puzzle. The elephant was therefore the aggregate of all perceptions. In the same vein, the consultant limits himself if all he is for instance is a financial expert. Without the knowledge of how finance, marketing and IT interact, you may be unable to provide wholesome advisory to your client.

I have consulted for a number of organizations that are their own albatross. A few years ago, an organization asked that I provide an outsourcing service. They needed thousands of workers on their 13,000-hectare plantation and factories. They confessed to having an extremely high worker attrition rate and needed a professional services firm to help. It was not long after I arrived on their expansive facility that I began to see parts of the problem: systemic discrimination against local workers that seeped into the pores of their operations. Foreigners lived in better conditions, had access to good transportation and all, while the locals lived under appalling conditions. Management, bogged down by the grinding challenges of running the operations couldn't see the structural defects in the system. As a consultant, you should have an eye for detail because the devil is usually in there.

For this type of organizational problem, a three-pronged approach that addresses the structure, policy and culture of the organization might optimize the system. The documentary cost of inefficiency fueled by sentiment makes no economic sense. The client may need proof of the cost of their structural delinquency. Be ready to provide hard facts. Afterall, facts that come from unbiased gathering and interpretation of data don't lie. Data integrity is key.

Key Learning Points

1. You can do more than you imagine
2. Develop a cross-functional perspective
3. Research success and failure cases in your client's industry
4. Stay abreast of the trends
5. Be agile

Action Plan

_____
_____
_____
_____
_____
_____
_____
_____
_____
_____
_____

Chapter Six: Don't Sell to Morons

"One of the important questions to ask in marketing is who?" – Maurice Ekpong

Don't sell to morons means simply that: don't sell to morons. In business, a moron is any person that isn't worth your time. You therefore have to be clear about your marketing strategy.

- Will you be focusing on small, medium or large corporates?
- What sectors will you target?
- What is the profile of the client you desire to serve?
- What geographical location or time zone can you serve effectively?

Like you may have inferred by now, you can't be everything to everyone. You have to be something to a select few. This is how you can be most effective as a consultant. Choose wisely and carefully.

There's this story of an old hunter in my village that saw six squirrels on a tree on one of his expeditions. Confused as to which one to target, he decided to kill all six from a single shot. He took a shot using his Dane gun while moving the gun from left to right. Of course, he had nothing to take home to his wife that evening!

We aren't talking of guns or hunting here although marketing your services may be akin to hunting for game. Remember the old adage that the secret of concentration is elimination? Focus is critical as it frees up resources for the highest value initiatives. To be honest, people sometimes may only be able to focus after trying their hands on several things. The test of the pudding is in the eating as they say. So, it may be okay to test different alternatives before settling on what works best for you.

Towards the end of 2012, two female entrepreneurs rang me up having been referred by an acquaintance. They had the idea of starting a world class family entertainment center (FEC), had drafted a concept note and business plan, but the potential foreign financiers needed documentary evidence that a market need existed for FECs in the country. I prepared a proposal that the client assented to and proceeded to conduct a market feasibility study across Lagos state over the next three months. The feasibility report enabled the clients secure funding for their idea of over two million dollars, setting up FECs in Lagos and Abuja Nigeria.

Entrepreneurs who willingly pay for professional market studies are not typical in some developing countries. Most will start a business on 'gut-feeling', without an assessment of market viability; especially when they are self-funding. Those who conduct market studies, do so to merely fulfil the requirement of financiers; lackadaisical of the merit in 'spending' money for studies or a business plan when it is self-evident that people will buy their intended product or service.

My advice to clients interested in starting a new business or launching a new product is to start with the market in view. This is smart advice. A product that appears to be selling now, may be in a mature or declining phase in its life cycle. Knowledge is power.

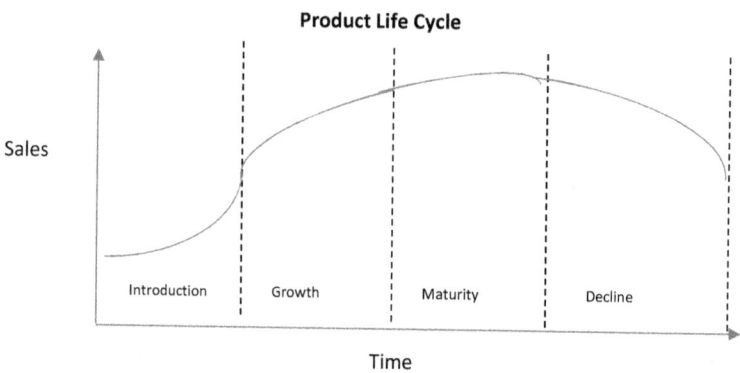

Figure 1 Above: Product Life Cycle

Also, a properly conducted market feasibility study will help in business planning.

- Carry out a detailed market research to understand the environment
- Identify your marketing objectives
- Segment your target market
- Define your services

- Work out the cost for implementing your plan and the corresponding reward you expect

Carry out a Detailed Market Research

Remember that it is okay to ask for help from subject matter experts if you don't have a particular skill. When planning any project, start with the market in view by asking the following questions:

- What do people need?
- How much of it do they need?
- At what price will they buy?
- What are the alternatives in the market now and in the pipeline?

Identify Your Marketing Objectives

Clarify in specific and measurable terms what you want to achieve.

- Define how you want your product or service perceived in the market
- What market share do you desire?
- By what time do you intend achieving this market share?
- What sort of margins do you intend making per unit product or service sold?

Define Your Target Market

- Who do you want to sell to?
- Where do you want to sell it?

Define Your Product or Service

- Why do we exist?

- What do we sell?
- When do we sell?
- To whom do we sell?
- How do we sell? Online, face-to-face, through third parties?

To prepare a business plan:

- Define your business
- Determine your target audience
- Understand the forces that shape your business
    - Existing competitors
    - Threat of new entrants
    - Alternatives or substitutes
    - Bargaining power of customers
    - Bargaining power of suppliers
- Create a competitive strategy
- Project your financial performance

Key Learning Points

1. You need to choose your clients carefully
2. Focus on what is most important
3. Always start with the market in view
4. Prepare a business plan
5. It's okay to ask for help

Action Plan

_____
_____
_____

Chapter Seven: Eat the Brains of Others

"Two good brains on a platter are better than one" – Maurice Ekpong

The brain is a complex organ that controls thought, memory, motor skills, look and feel and every other process that regulates the human body. Combined, the brain and spinal cord that extends from it make up the central nervous system.

The human brain beats any super computer with an incredible ability to process, store and retrieve information in milliseconds. Indeed, the brain is an engineering marvel. According to some estimates by Ashley Feinberg in an article published August 6, 2013 on GIZMODO titled *'An 83,000-Processor Supercomputer Can Only Match About 1% of Your Brain,* "you've undoubtedly heard over and over again about what an absurdly complex entity the human brain is. But a new breakthrough by Japanese and German scientists might finally drive the point home. Taking advantage of the almost 83,000 processors of one of the world's most powerful supercomputers, the team was able to mimic just one percent of one second's worth of human brain activity – and even that took 40 minutes."

While this isn't intended as a lecture on neuroscience, the point of the tremendous power of the human brain cannot be overemphasized. This point is especially important in consulting, considering that the consultant in a way seeks to improve organizational performance through thought leadership.

There are indeed times when the consultants' thoughts are foggy due to any one or combination of factors including fatigue, stress, illness or just having a bad day. These factors come unannounced and have no respect for project deadlines. In this situation, "eating the brains of others" can help. Note that I am not advocating cannibalism here. Rather, I am talking about building and taking advantage of relationships with subject matter experts that can give your brain the required 'spark' through brainstorming.

Science indicates though, that at any point in time, your brain is constantly eating itself. In a report published October 29, 2021 on BBCs Science Focus, neuroscientist Dean Burnett explains the brains gruesome method for spring cleaning. Said he: "Phagocytosis is a process whereby cells will envelop and consume smaller cells or molecules. In order to remove them from the system, it's basically cells eating other cells, or substances. Our immune system is based on this; dedicated white blood cells consume pathogens, thus getting rid of them and their disruptive influence on our bodies. A lot of phagocytosis is happening in the brain, at any given time. While keeping pathogens and other invaders out is obviously very important, phagocytosis is happening, just to keep the brain running as is".

Concluding, Burnett reports that "our brains aren't static. They're flexible, adaptable, constantly reacting to what life throws at them. That's largely the source of their power. But they wouldn't be able to do this if they weren't willing to eat parts of themselves on a regular basis."

Depending on the assignment at hand, pressure for deadlines etcetera, the consultant can go days on end with very little sleep. As a previous advisor to a Fortune Global 500 multinational food and agribusiness conglomerate headquartered in Singapore, I have conducted extensive market studies for the oil palm and rubber value chains, negotiating brownfield and Greenfield opportunities for them.

These assignments required that my team and I traverse the entire country gathering data and speaking with different stakeholders. For days on end, I could go without a lot of sleep preparing for meetings and presentations with executive management teams visiting from Singapore. The pressure usually pays off in the end after an excellent job is done. In the thick of things however, the challenge may not be very pretty.

As a management consultant, different curve balls will be thrown at you, tasking your brain to the point where it may begin to eat itself. You should be able to eat the brains of others to make up for parts of your own brain that your own brain may have eaten!

The idea of eating other people's brains is by no means preposterous. Even some of the brightest people in history at one point or the other used other people's ideas. Ask Jeff

Williams, an intellectual property lawyer who thinks that 5 times in history when an idea was stolen include:

- *Thomas Edison and the light bulb*
- *Albert Einstein and the Theory of Relativity*
- *Alexander Graham Bell and the Telephone*
- *Alexander Fleming and Penicillin*
- *Galileo Galilee and the Telescope*

Although Nikola Tesla who earlier in his career apprenticed with Edison didn't say so, some people have the notion that Edison may have eaten the brain of Tesla in his patent of the light bulb. There is a caveat here. I am not even remotely promoting theft of intellectual property. That, my friend, is a no-go area. Fact is, the best brains brainstorm with others. The idea I am promoting is of two or more people cooperating to produce more than each individual could have done on their own. The cosmos supports such collaboration, often rewarding them with resounding success. You will do well to eat the brains of others!

Key Learning Points

1. Two good brains are better than one
2. Prepare to deal with pressure
3. Brainstorm

Action Plan

_____
_____
_____
_____
_____
_____

Chapter Eight: Go Against the Grain

"Why not go out on a limb? Isn't that where the fruit is?" – Frank Scully

On fruit trees, you often find the most luscious fruits on the limbs. If you must get them, you must risk climbing. In a similar vein, the management consultant's success will ultimately be directly proportional to their risk appetite. A risk averse consultant will struggle with the crowd for low hanging fruits. The ambitious consultant will blaze the trail; creating new frontiers where angels dare to tread.

I believe new vistas for exploits in the consulting space are unfolding. There is no limit to what the human mind can conceive and what the human hands can create. If you can think it, you can do it. To make impact as a consultant, you must be willing to question age-old assumptions. Just because it has been done a certain way for eons doesn't mean it cannot be improved upon.

The new frontier in consultancy will be created by people willing to challenge the status quo. Great floods sometime start from little droplets of water. The key is consistency. Keeping at it without looking back except to check for alignment with core principles.

In his inaugural address, former US President Jimmy Carter quoted his high school teacher Miss Julia Coleman as saying "we must adjust to changing times while holding to unchanging principles." So, principles and core values like integrity, respect, confidentiality etcetera are supposed to be unchanging. But the way work is done must constantly evolve to match environmental, social and technological advances.

One person that exemplifies this spirit of breaking new frontiers and perhaps the greatest inventor so far, this 21st century, is Elon Musk. Through sheer imagination, Elon founded SpaceX in 2002 convinced that humanity can become a multiplanet species. He has designed and built rockets at a fraction of the cost of long-established competitors including Boeing. What Elon is doing in technology, you can do in consulting with the caveat that you will need the discipline of Elon to match his incredible work rate.

At least, the starting point is desire. You don't need money to buy desire, but can ignite it from reading the biographies of people like Elon and a multitude of others you admire. Desire is the takeoff point for vision. A desire for instance to make a difference among the world's homeless or poor can lead you into development consulting. While you may not presently have the requisite qualification or experience, a vision fueled by desire for change can galvanize you to pursue the knowledge and develop the skill sets to actualize your dreams.

Craig Handley dreamed of meeting Sir Richard Branson. When Branson had a speaking engagement at the Direct Marketing Association in San Francisco, Craig dressed up as security to get backstage. He walked up to Branson with a $20 bill wrapped around his business card, shook his hand and said "this is the first $20 we are going to make together". It worked like magic as he had immediate impact on Branson with whom he has had a relationship in the years after.

Nelson Mandela. Wrongly imprisoned for 27 years for fighting against apartheid and after his release and upon becoming President of South Africa, refused to pay his incarcerators in their own coin, choosing against the grain to forgive in the interest of his country. This singular act won him the Nobel Peace Prize in 1993 earning him the stature of one of the most influential persons of the 20th century.

Mary Slessor. Scottish missionary born 2 December 1848, worked tirelessly and at the risk of her own life among the Efik people in present day Calabar Nigeria to stop the killing of twins from entrenched witchcraft and superstition. Human sacrifice routinely accompanied the death of an important person and the ritual murder of twins was of repugnance to Mary. Her work immortalized her among the people she served who still revere her to date.

The aforementioned are stories of real people who chose the path less traveled, and are celebrated for doing so today. As a consultant, you will not be remembered for doing the routine. Going the extra mile or against the grain will put you at the top of the food chain. If you are anywhere but at the top of the chain, you and your work will be confined by higher-order species to the dustbin of history.

Key Learning Points

1. Be an outlier
2. Question the status quo
3. Remember that principles and values never change
4. Let desire drive your vision

Action Plan

Chapter Nine: Have a Long-Term Perspective

"Right now, slips by into the past. As long as there is a tomorrow there is hope" – Maurice Ekpong

The world is becoming increasingly short-termist. Patience is almost a lost virtue as today's microwave generation pursues gratification. Pursuit of gratification has become a societal cancer, upending generations of common-sense stability at the individual, organizational, national and global levels. In the final analysis, a long-term perspective is what will distinguish between organizations that survive the complexities of present-day cultural suicide missions, and future market leadership.

The consultant must resist the allure of short-term gratification especially if it truncates or imperils the client's ability to visualize and win at the end zone. You must therefore carefully weigh all available evidence to appropriately advise your client on the right course of action to take per time. Never rush decision making, but do it carefully and thoughtfully. Having decided, have enough slack to change course and avoid shipwreck while keeping an eye on the long-term goal.

I was recently invited by a multinational to Chair an international conference in an East African country. I agreed to chair the conference without asking them to pay for the service. At the end of the conference, the hosts were very pleased, informing me of a desire to work out long term partnership, requesting I let them know if I needed anything. I thanked them for the opportunity but refused to ask for any reward when I returned back to Lagos. I am more inclined to building long term relationships than I am in short term rewards.

To be sure, there is nothing wrong with getting paid for rendering an excellent service such as I did at the conference. I routinely receive payment for services rendered. The point is, we can discern when an opportunity is availed us to trade in short term gratification for longer term benefits. Given a choice between the two, always think long-term.

On one forum for policy development that I belong, current discourse has hinged on the ominous clouds over some developing countries. It is clear that no matter the policy formulated to reverse poverty, create jobs, or craft a vision for the common good, crooks in positions of power subvert same for personal aggrandizement. In other words, they trade the future of their countries for immediate selfish benefit. A frustrated individual asked a desperate question: "how can such countries achieve national values reset?". As ominous as the signs appear, I argue that the biggest challenge facing some countries is the indifference of good people, who sit down and do nothing.

I have an analogy from basic physics explaining why I think some countries remain the way they are in spite of having many people with good intentions. First of all, good intentions don't amount to much in the real world. To be effective, good intentions must be matched with action.

In physics, we learn that energy cannot be created or destroyed but can be stored in different forms. One way to store it is in the form of chemical energy in a battery. When connected in a circuit, a battery can produce electricity.

A battery has two ends: a positive terminal (cathode) and a negative terminal (anode). If you connect the two terminals with a wire, a circuit is formed. Electrons will flow from the anode to the cathode through the wire and a current of electricity is produced. Batteries can be stored for a long time and still work because the chemical process doesn't start until the electrons flow from the negative terminal to the positive terminal through a circuit.

The cathode are the good guys while the anode represents the kleptomaniacs, who don't mind burning down the house with everyone including themselves inside because they think they can make money from the ashes. I find that the greatest tragedy is that the good guys talk about it, but seldom get to confront the bad guys, thereby short circuiting the change process.

Margaret Mead, the American Cultural Anthropologist once said: "Never doubt that a small group of thoughtful, committed citizens can change the world; indeed, it's the only thing that ever has." To this, one person 'infamously' replied me... "We do not doubt you. Everyone has seen how a few thoughtful, committed men have turned" our countries into wastelands.

Short-termism destroys nations and institutions. For social transformation projects particularly in poverty stricken third world countries, it is important to consider building an inclusive economic empowerment model. When pressure to meet basic needs is removed from the equation, it becomes practicable and sustainable to plan with stakeholders for the long term.

Key Learning Points

1. Delay gratification
2. Think long-term
3. Create a sustainable system that supports long-term thinking

Action Plan

_____
_____
_____
_____
_____
_____
_____
_____
_____
_____
_____
_____
_____

Chapter Ten: Toolkit for Consultants

If you still feel like management consultancy is for you after reading the previous nine chapters, congratulations! Here are a few tools that can help you get started with diagnosing organizational problems whilst evaluating potential solutions. Note that this is not an exhaustive list. You will find other resources along the way:

Methodologies

In the course of consulting, you are very likely to encounter similar challenges. To boost your productivity, it is fitting that you build and maintain a database of standardized approaches to organizational problems. For starters, you may want to create this database with a spreadsheet. You can categorize different problems and capture how it was approached. The following template can guide:

Category / Industry	Problem	Resources utilized	Project Timelines	Challenges Encountered	Solution proffered	Key Learning Points
ICT						
Media						
Manufacturing						
Wellness						
Real Estate						
Fashion						
Nonprofits						
Insurance						
Sanitation						
Hospitality						
Tourism						

Table 1 above: Methodology Template

Modelling

- Visualize your model on a single sheet of paper
- Keep it simple
- Prepare a storyboard
- Prioritize clarity
- Remember that your model is a means to an end
- The model must fit the business story

Business Model Template

The business model canvas below can help you. The canvas was originally proposed by Swiss business theorist and entrepreneur Alexander Osterwalder as part of his Ph.D. research.

Key Partnerships	Key Activities	Value Proposition	Customer Relationships	Customer Segments
	Key Resources		Channels	
Cost Structure		Revenue Streams		

Figure 2 above: The Business Model Canvas

Interviewing

Remember that job interviews differ from interviews seeking information
- Prepare an issue map that captures the following:
    - What information do I seek?
    - Who is my target audience?
    - Where are they located?
    - How can I best reach them?
- Make sure to keep the client informed
- Prepare adequate logistics
- Practice before D-day
- Arrive venue in time

Interview Guide

Preparing for the Interview	
If meeting face-to-face • Be clean and appropriately dressed • Have writing material and a prepared question guide • Thank the interviewee for the time • Ask questions and write down answers • At the end of the session, thank the interviewee again	If meeting over the phone or online • Be in a room free from noise and distractions • Have prepared questions and writing materials • Thank the interviewee for the time • Ask questions and write down the answers • At the end of the session thank the interviewee again

Table 2 above: Interview Guide

Process Mapping

A process map is a planning and management tool that visually describes the work flow. It typically a series of events leading up to an end result.

For example, to bake bread, the process map can be:

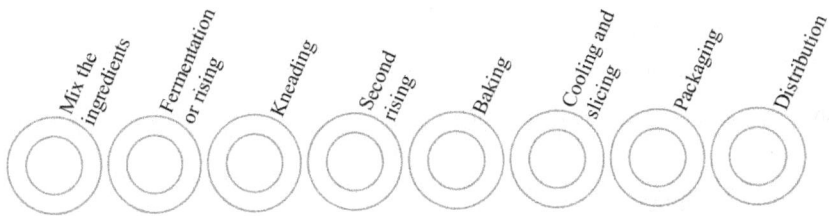

Figure 3 above: Process map for making bread

Guide for Process Mapping

Questions to Ask	Key Issues
Who?	Identify decision makers, other stakeholders likely to be impacted
What?	List activities, information flows etc.
Why?	Define value created or intended
How?	Determine scope of each process, its steps until final outcome is achieved

Table 3 above: Guide for process mapping

Performance Management

Performance management is really performance measurement. What you cannot measure you cannot manage. Measurement can be done of organizational structures, people and processes.

To create a performance management system:

- Set clear goals and objectives
- Identify and implement a performance appraisal system
- Allow for self-evaluation (in case of evaluating people)
- Gather data and provide feedback
- Discuss career or organizational development goals
- Make room for feedback
- Review and update periodically

Performance Management Framework

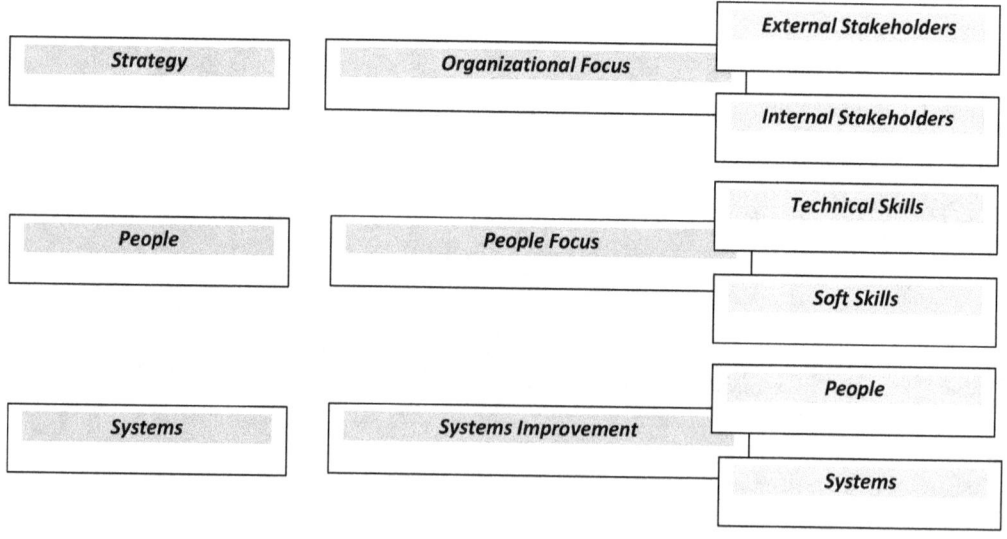

Figure 4 above: Performance Management Framework

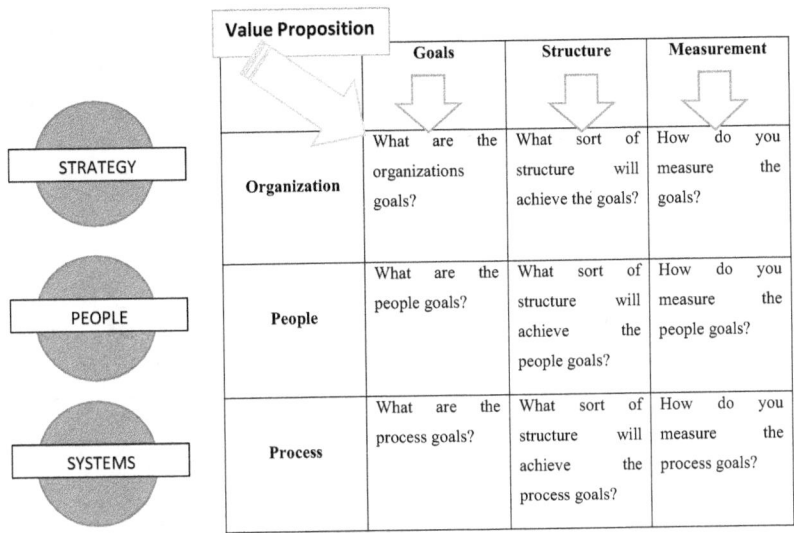

Figure 5 above: High-level Performance Management Framework

Below: Employee Performance Management Template

Goals Achieved:		Review. Next Review:	Comments:	
Factors	Excellent	Good	Average	Poor
Work quality	☐	☐	☐	☐
Innovation	☐	☐	☐	☐
Productivity	☐	☐	☐	☐
Technical skills	☐	☐	☐	☐
Team work	☐	☐	☐	☐
Initiative	☐	☐	☐	☐
Knowledge	☐	☐	☐	☐
Punctuality	☐	☐	☐	☐

Figure 6 above: Employee performance management

Action Plan

Appendix I.   **Bibliography**

EHEC 0104:H4 in Germany 2011: Large outbreak of bloody diarrhea and haemolytic uraemic syndrome by shiga toxin-producing E-Coli via contaminated food; Reinhard Burger; National Academies Press (US); 2012

Aircraft accident report, Korean Air flight 801, National Transportation Safety Board, 1997

https://www.reuters.com/world/europe/several-injured-roller-coaster-accident-sweden-2023-06-25/

Code of Ethical Professional Conduct for IMC Members and CMCS, IMC-Nigeria 2024

Six Blind Men and the Elephant, John Godfrey Saxe, 1873

Acres of Diamonds, Russel Conwell; 1890

The Ethical Dilemmas Behind the 2008 Global Financial Crisis, Elisa Desousa; 2020

https://www.britannica.com/event/indian-ocean-tsunami-of-2004

https://www.txpatentattorney.com/blog/5-times-in-history-when-an-idea-was-stolen/

An 83,000-Processor Supercomputer Can Only Match About 1% of Your Brain, GIZMODO Ashley Feinberg, August 6, 2013

https://www.sciencefocus.com/the-human-body/does-the-brain-eat-itself

Appendix II.   **List of Figures and Tables**

Description	Page
Figure 1, Product Life Cycle	28
Figure 2, The Business Model Canvas	41
Figure 3, Process Map for Making Bread	43
Figure 4, Performance Management Framework	44
Figure 5, High-level Performance Management Framework	45
Figure 6, Employee Performance Management Template	45
Table 1, Methodology Template	40
Table 2, Interview Guide	42
Table 3, Guide for Process Mapping	43

About the Author

Maurice Ekpong is a Fellow of the Institute of Management Consultants (IMC-Nigeria) and a Certified Management Consultant (CMC).

He is one of the best multidisciplinary experts from Africa, and an inspiring, multidisciplinary and results-oriented business leader with over 22 years' experience providing best-in-class business development, research, market intelligence and projects planning and development services across a wide array of sectors spanning agriculture, finance, healthcare, education and infrastructure development.

He has extensive experience in consultancy and building Business to Business (B2B), Business to Government (B2G) and Business to Customer (B2C) relationships with multinational and multilateral organizations from Europe, Asia and across Africa with meticulous and successful business execution.

Maurice is an international conference chair and speaker, and an analyst, researcher and writer on television, newspaper and major development journals.

Between 2016 and 2019, he was appointed by Government to the Board of the Cross River State Agriculture and Food Technology Agency. He is also a founding Board Member at Maurana and an advisor to executive management teams in Africa and around the world.

In addition, Maurice is a policy and development expert, a certified international mediator and an African Research Councilor with the Wheeler Institute for Business and Development of the London Business School.

www.ingramcontent.com/pod-product-compliance
Lightning Source LLC
Chambersburg PA
CBHW072054230526
45479CB00010B/1053